T0027079

SOJOURNER TRUTH

BY HEATHER MOORE NIVER

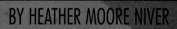
Gareth Stevens
PUBLISHING

Please visit our website, www.garethstevens.com. For a free color catalog of all our high-quality books, call toll free 1-800-542-2595 or fax 1-877-542-2596.

Library of Congress Cataloging-in-Publication Data

Niver, Heather Moore.
Sojourner Truth / Heather Moore Niver.
    pages cm. — (Heroes of Black history)
Includes bibliographical references and index.
ISBN 978-1-4824-2912-1 (pbk.)
ISBN 978-1-4824-2913-8 (6 pack)
ISBN 978-1-4824-2914-5 (library binding)
 . Truth, Sojourner, -1883—Juvenile literature. 2. African American abolitionists—Biography—Juvenile literature. 3. African American women—Biography—Juvenile literature. 4. Abolitionists—United States—Biography—Juvenile literature. 5. Social reformers—United States—Biography—Juvenile literature. I. Title.
E185.97.T8N58 2015
306.3'62092—dc23
[B]
                                    2015006057

First Edition

Published in 2016 by
Gareth Stevens Publishing
 11 East 14th Street, Suite 349
New York, NY 10003

Copyright © 2016 Gareth Stevens Publishing

Designer: Katelyn E. Reynolds
Editor: Therese Shea

Photo credits: Cover, p. 1 (Sojourner Truth), cover, pp. 1–32 (background image) Hulton Archive/Getty Images; p. 5 Randall Studio/National Portrait Gallery, Smithsonian Institution/Wikipedia.org; p. 7 SUNY New Paltz Sojourner Truth Library/Wikipedia.org; p. 8 © iStockphoto.com/PeterJSeager; p. 9 Gyrobo/Wikipedia.org; pp. 11, 12, 15 Corinne Nyquist, SUNY New Paltz; pp. 13, 17 Library of Congress; p. 19 Photograph by George K. Warren (d. 1884) /Wikipedia.org; pp. 21, 23 MPI/Getty Images; p. 25 Universal History Archive/Getty Images; p. 27 Gladstone Collection, Prints and Photographs Division, Library of Congress/Wikipedia.org; p. 28 (bust) Architect of the Capitol (www.aoc.gov); p. 28 (photo) Chip Somodevilla/Getty Images.

All rights reserved. No part of this book may be reproduced in any form without permission in writing from the publisher, except by a reviewer.

Printed in the United States of America

CPSIA compliance information: Batch #CS15GS: For further information contact Gareth Stevens, New York, New York at 1-800-542-2595.

CONTENTS

Words in the glossary appear in **bold** type the first time they are used in the text.

SOJOURNER FOR JUSTICE

Some say Sojourner Truth was the most famous African American of the 19th century. When she died, it's believed that more than 1,000 people attended her funeral.

This peaceful **activist** stood up for the rights of blacks in America and also for women of all races. In fact, Truth said that the two issues were connected. She spent 40 years traveling all over the United States, speaking out for equal rights. She was known for her humor, songs, and sharp tongue, and she wasn't afraid to use any of them. She spent her life working for justice.

WHAT'S IN A NUMBER?

In Battle Creek, Michigan, Sojourner Truth's tombstone says she died at the age of 105! During her life, Truth enjoyed letting people guess how old she was. She also liked being known as "the world's oldest **lecturer**." But based on historical information, she was probably about 86 years old when she died.

After an extraordinary life of travel, Sojourner Truth settled in Battle Creek, Michigan. She was buried there in Oak Hill Cemetery.

5

SLAVE DAYS

Sojourner Truth was born about 1797 near Swartekill in Ulster County, New York. Then called Isabella Baumfree, she was the daughter of slave parents from Africa. Her father was from Ghana, and her mother's parents were from Guinea. When Isabella was just 9 years old, her owner died. The young girl was sold with a flock of sheep to a new master for $100.

Isabella was sold two more times, until she finally became a slave of John Dumont in West Park, New York. She had grown up speaking only Dutch and first learned to speak English in West Park.

LOVE AND MARRIAGE

Around 1815, Isabella met and fell in love with Robert, a slave on a nearby farm. However, slaves couldn't marry whomever they wanted. Robert's master prevented them from seeing each other again, since he wouldn't own any children they had together. In 1817, John Dumont made her marry an older slave named Thomas. Isabella had five children.

6

Isabella's life began in a Dutch-settled area of New York. Although she learned to speak English and Dutch, she never learned to read or write. This was the house of her first owner, Colonel Johannes Hardenbergh.

7

FINALLY, FREEDOM!

Both John Dumont and his wife Sally were very cruel. A New York antislavery law was passed that gradually emancipated, or freed, slaves beginning July 4, 1827. Isabella and Thomas asked Dumont to emancipate them a year before this, promising to work twice as much. He agreed, but when the time came, he broke his word. Dumont claimed an injury of Isabella's had slowed her down, and she hadn't worked hard enough.

Isabella was **frustrated**, so she prayed for guidance. She decided to escape with her youngest daughter, Sophia. Thomas chose to stay behind with the other children.

PROMISE BROKEN

Isabella worked even after she badly injured her hand. Dumont used her injured hand as an excuse to deny her freedom. To gain freedom, she did all her work and some extra. She even spun 100 pounds (45 kg) of wool, even after John Dumont broke his promise.

8

Isabella said, "I did not run off, for I thought that wicked, but I walked off, believing that to be all right." This bridge is located in Sojourner Truth Park in the area of New York where she spent her early years.

9

"SOJOURNER'S JOURNEY BEGINS"

Isabella didn't wait until the cover of darkness to escape. She later told her former master, "I did not run away, I walked away by daylight." Taking only a few supplies and some clothes, she walked more than 10 miles (16 km). Finally, she arrived at the home of Isaac and Maria Van Wagenen. They didn't believe in slavery.

That night, Dumont found her and demanded she return. Isabella refused. The Van Wagenens gave him $20 to leave Isabella alone and $5 for Sophia. He took the money and left. Isabella lived very happily with the Van Wagenens for a time.

WALKING IN HER FOOTSTEPS

Today, you can walk some of the same roads Isabella is believed to have traveled on her road to freedom. Although some highways have paved over the original roads, many of the dirt trails still exist in Ulster County, New York. The Sojourner Truth Freedom Trail is 11.5 miles (18.5 km) long.

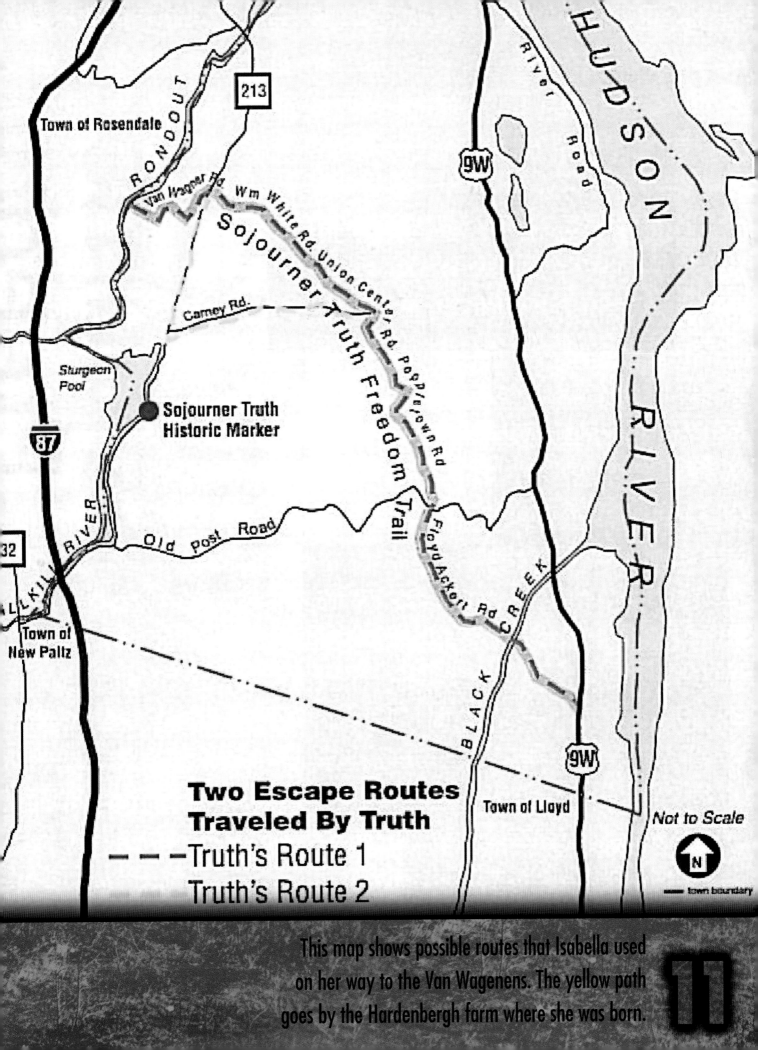

Two Escape Routes Traveled By Truth

– – – Truth's Route 1

Truth's Route 2

This map shows possible routes that Isabella used on her way to the Van Wagenens. The yellow path goes by the Hardenbergh farm where she was born.

IN A FLASH OF LIGHTNING

Isabella was very grateful to the Van Wagenens. She even took their last name for a time. Her life was so much better, but she missed her family at the Dumont farm. In fact, she was tempted to go back and celebrate a holiday called Pinkster with them.

But before she made a decision, Isabella said that "with the suddenness of a flash of lightning" she had a vision of Jesus. She believed she was being told not to go. She also felt she was given the strength to resist going back to her old life.

FAITH IN THE FOREST

Isabella didn't have much contact with other blacks during her time at the Dumont farm. To help deal with loneliness, she built a little "temple" of her own out of branches in the woods. Here she prayed and talked to God about her terrible situation. Religion became a large part of her life.

Van Wagenen house

12

Isabella's mother may have taught her about the
African tradition of building stick shacks as "temples."

13

STANDING UP FOR HER SON

In 1826, Isabella learned some shocking news. Dumont had illegally sold her 5-year-old son Peter into slavery in Alabama. Alabama had no law that would free him as in New York.

Isabella decided to fight for her son. She raised the funds she needed to take her case to an Ulster County court. This was one of the first cases in the United States in which a black woman took a white man to court—and won! Peter was returned to his mother in 1828. It was Isabella's first step toward activism.

STRIKING SOJOURNER!

Isabella, later known as Sojourner Truth, was a woman people noticed and remembered. She stood almost 6 feet (1.8 m) tall. She spoke English with a low, ringing voice, but had a heavy Dutch **accent**. When she sang, even an angry crowd would be calmed. She was also known for having a great sense of humor.

Isabella saved her son from a life of slavery by going to court in the Ulster County Courthouse, which still stands today.

15

A NEW START IN NEW YORK CITY

In the late 1820s, Isabella moved to New York City. First, she worked as a household servant for **evangelist** Elijah Pierson. Then, she worked for Robert Matthews, who called himself **Prophet** Matthias. Isabella lived in his community outside New York City—the Kingdom of Matthias—from 1833 to 1834. Unfortunately, Matthews was dishonest and mistreated Isabella.

After leaving Matthews and returning to New York City, Isabella decided to be a preacher. Through her speaking appearances, she got to know women's rights supporters and **abolitionists**. As she learned more about these subjects, she began to include her opinions about them in her talks.

ACCUSED!

Not long after Isabella left Pierson's household, he died. Matthews was accused of poisoning him, supposedly for money. A married couple from the Kingdom of Matthias, the Folgers, accused Isabella of helping Matthews. Sojourner stood up for herself. She took the Folgers to court for slander, or lying about her, and won!

Isabella moved back to New York City in 1835 and lived there until 1843.

17

TRUTH AT LAST

Isabella began to feel she had to leave New York City. She told friends, "The Spirit calls me [East], and I must go." Around the same time, she decided to change her name to Sojourner Truth. This name reflected her new life as a traveling preacher who spoke out for truth and justice. She headed to Massachusetts.

In 1844, Truth joined the Northampton Association for Education and Industry, a group of people living and working together who believed in equal rights for everyone. Here she met Frederick Douglass, the famous black abolitionist. She also met Olive Gilbert, who would become a very close friend and later write Truth's life story.

SETTING SAIL

After his rescue from slavery, Peter lived with his mother for a time. In 1839, he went to work on the *Zone of Nantucket*, a whaling ship. Over 2 years, Sojourner Truth received three letters from her son. However, he wasn't on the ship when it returned in 1842. She never heard from him again.

Frederick Douglass was an ex-slave, like Sojourner Truth. After running away, he purchased his freedom and started an antislavery newspaper.

19

PLAINLY FOR PEACE

Frederick Douglass admired Truth's way with words as she preached, but he looked down on her for not being more educated. As usual, Truth stood up for herself. She used her plain and simple language to argue her opinions with him.

In 1852, the two were at a meeting at which Douglass challenged blacks to use force to gain freedom. Truth disagreed. As he finished his speech, she simply asked Douglass, "Is God gone?" She felt that more peaceful action was a better route. From then on, Truth was known for her faith in nonviolence.

SUPPORTING HERSELF

Truth never learned to read or write. However, she told her friend Olive Gilbert her life story, and Gilbert wrote it down. Together, they published *The Narrative of Sojourner Truth* in 1850. Truth traveled around the East and Midwest, singing, preaching, and **debating**. She made enough money to buy herself a house.

SOJOURNER TRUTH.

NARRATIVE

OF

SOJOURNER TRUTH,

A

NORTHERN SLAVE,

EMANCIPATED FROM BODILY SERVITUDE BY THE STATE OF

NEW YORK, IN 1828.

WITH A PORTRAIT.

'SWEET is the virgin honey, though the wild bee store it in a reed;
And bright the jewelled band that circleth an Ethiop's arm;
Pure are the grains of gold in the turbid stream of the Ganges;
And fair the living flowers that spring from the dull cold sod.
Wherefore, thou gentle student, bend thine ear to my speech,
For I also am as thou art; our hearts can commune together:
To meanest matters will I stoop, for mean is the lot of mortal;
I will rise to noblest themes, for the soul hath a heritage of glory.'

NEW YORK
PUBLIC

BOSTON:

PRINTED FOR THE AUTHOR.

1850.

AIN'T I A WOMAN?

In 1851, Sojourner Truth gave one of the most famous women's rights and abolitionist speeches of all time in Akron, Ohio. Speaking to the Women's Rights **Convention**, she said:

"That man over there says that women need to be helped into carriages, and lifted over ditches, and to have the best place everywhere. Nobody ever helps me into carriages, or over mud-puddles, or gives me any best place! And ain't I a woman? Look at me! Look at my arm! I have ploughed and planted, and gathered into barns, and no man could head [beat] me! And ain't I a woman?"

Truth tore down reasons why people felt women shouldn't have the same rights as men in this speech, later titled "Ain't I a Woman?"

A CALM TRUTH

Truth's audience wasn't always filled with supporters. In 1858, someone in an audience in Indiana began **heckling** Truth while she spoke. He shouted out that the very tall Truth must be a man. She stayed calm, as always, and began to talk about her very real and very hard past as a slave woman and mother.

22

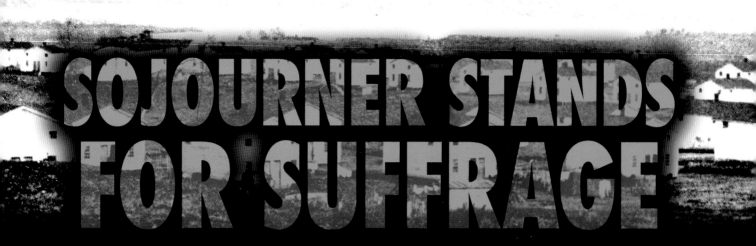

SOJOURNER STANDS FOR SUFFRAGE

Sojourner Truth did a lot more than give speeches. During the American Civil War (1861–1865), she successfully fought for blacks to be able to become soldiers. She then helped collect supplies for black troops.

Truth also got to know women such as Susan B. Anthony and Elizabeth Cady Stanton, who were working toward women's suffrage, or the right to vote. The women didn't agree on everything, though, especially when Anthony and Stanton put the rights of women ahead of the rights of blacks. Many people in the suffrage movement felt they had to choose between suffrage for black men and suffrage for women.

PRESIDENTIAL POPULARITY

In 1864, Truth got the opportunity to meet President Abraham Lincoln at the White House. She called him the "best president ever." She admitted to Lincoln that she had never heard of him before he became president. He told her he had known about her for many years. Later on, Truth also met Presidents Andrew Johnson and Ulysses S. Grant.

24

Truth's friend Frances Titus may have commissioned the painting of Lincoln showing Truth a Bible that the black community of Baltimore, Maryland, gave him.

25

CIVIL WAR CELEBRITY

As the Civil War raged on, Sojourner Truth became even more popular. Harriet Beecher Stowe wrote an article about Truth in 1863 for *Atlantic Monthly* magazine. Other people were talking and writing about her, too. Anyone interested in rights for blacks and women knew her name.

Sojourner Truth had a hand in her own publicity, too. She sold *cartes de visite* (KAHRT DUH vee-ZEET), which were cards that included her photograph and the words: "I Sell the Shadow to Support the Substance." Historians think she meant she was selling a picture of herself (the Shadow) to support her actual self and her work for equality (the Substance).

ANOTHER WIN

In 1865, a law was passed in Washington, DC, that stated that it was illegal to refuse blacks rides on horse-drawn streetcars. Still, most blacks were too scared to ride, but not Sojourner Truth. After a **conductor** refused her a ride and pushed her, Truth had the man arrested. She took him to court and won!

26

I Sell the Shadow to Support the Substance.

SOJOURNER TRUTH.

Cartes de visite were a European custom that came to the United States about 1859. It was popular to give them out to friends.

A LEGENDARY LADY

Sojourner Truth's life ended at her home in Battle Creek, Michigan, on November 26, 1883. Her work is still remembered today, though. She was included in the National Women's Hall of Fame in Seneca Falls, New York, in 1981. In 1986, she was featured on a postage stamp.

In 2009, a **bust** of Truth was placed in Emancipation Hall in the US Capitol. About 1,000 people were there to celebrate her life. Hillary Clinton, the secretary of state at the time, said that Truth was finally taking "her rightful place alongside the heroes who have helped shape our nation's history."

TIMELINE OF
THE LIFE OF SOJOURNER TRUTH

1797 Isabella Baumfree is born in Ulster County, New York.

1810 John Dumont buys Isabella.

1815 Isabella meets Robert, a neighboring slave.

1826 Isabella walks to freedom with her daughter Sophia.

1827 New York's antislavery law comes into effect.

1828 Isabella wins a court case to get her son Peter out of slavery in Alabama.

1843 Isabella changes her name to Sojourner Truth.

1850 *The Narrative of Sojourner Truth* is published.

1851 Truth delivers her most famous speech, later called "Ain't I a Woman?"

1864 Truth meets President Abraham Lincoln at the White House.

1865 Truth fights for black rights by riding a streetcar in Washington, DC.

1883 Sojourner Truth dies at her home in Battle Creek, Michigan.

GLOSSARY

abolitionist: one who fights to end slavery

accent: a way of saying words that occurs among the people of a particular place

activist: one who acts strongly in support of or against an issue

bust: a sculpture of a person's head, neck, and upper body

conductor: a person who collects money or tickets from passengers

convention: a gathering of people who have a common interest or purpose

debate: to argue or publicly discuss

evangelist: a person who tries to convince people to become Christian

frustrated: feeling angry, discouraged, or upset because of not being able to do something

heckle: to shout insults in order to disturb someone giving a speech or performance

lecturer: someone who gives a speech about a certain topic

prophet: a member of some religions who is thought to deliver messages from God

FOR MORE INFORMATION

BOOKS

Housel, Debra J. *Sojourner Truth: A Path to Freedom.* Huntington Beach, CA: Teacher Created Materials, 2011.

Spinale, Laura. *Sojourner Truth.* Mankato, MN: The Child's World, 2009.

WEBSITES

Biography: Sojourner Truth
www.ducksters.com/history/civil_rights/sojourner_truth.php
Learn important dates in Sojourner Truth's life.

The Narrative of Sojourner Truth
xroads.virginia.edu/~Hyper/Truth/cover.html
Visit this site to read Truth's life story as told to Olive Gilbert.

Sojourner Truth
www.nps.gov/wori/historyculture/sojourner-truth.htm
Read the entire "Ain't I a Woman?" speech here.

Publisher's note to educators and parents: Our editors have carefully reviewed these websites to ensure that they are suitable for students. Many websites change frequently, however, and we cannot guarantee that a site's future contents will continue to meet our high standards of quality and educational value. Be advised that students should be closely supervised whenever they access the Internet.

INDEX